BOOK ANALYSIS

By Georgina Murphy

A Farewell to Arms

BY ERNEST HEMINGWAY

ERNEST HEMINGWAY

- **Born in Oak Park, Illinois in 1899.**
- **Died in Ketchum, Idaho in 1961.**
- **Notable works:**
  - *The Sun Also Rises* (1926), early Modernist novel
  - *For Whom the Bell Tolls* (1940), war novel
  - *The Complete Short Stories of Ernest Hemingway* (1987), posthumous collection

Ernest Hemingway is regarded as one of the first and most influential American Modernists. Between 1920 and the mid-1950s, he published seven novels, six short story collections and two works of non-fiction. In 1953 he won the Pulitzer Prize for Fiction for his last major work of fiction, *The Old Man and the Sea* (1952), and in 1954 he was awarded the Nobel Prize for Literature.

Hemingway is remembered for his use of the 'iceberg theory', an economical, minimalist style alternatively known as the 'theory of omission'.

As he writes in *Death in the Afternoon*, "the dignity of movement of an iceberg is due to only one-eighth of it being above water" (1999: 154). By focusing on surface elements of the story (just "one-eighth"), Hemingway believed that the underlying significance of the narrative could shine through more poignantly and powerfully, despite not being obviously referred to. As Hemingway's iceberg style aims to capture the truth, his novels are considered to be works of realism. Thematically, Hemingway often uses the setting of war to examine the effects of conflict on human love, lust, fear, loss, guilt and betrayal.

A FAREWELL TO ARMS

WAR NOVEL WITH A ROMANCE NARRATIVE

- **Genre:** novel
- **Reference edition:** Hemingway, E. (1994) *A Farewell to Arms*. Berlin: Arrow Books.
- **1st edition:** 1929
- **Themes:** war, love, conflict, politics, illness, romance, family, friendship, loss

A Farewell to Arms is widely regarded as a product of Hemingway's own time serving as a soldier in the First World War, when in 1918, he was recruited as an ambulance driver for the Italian Red Cross. Whilst serving on the Austrian-Italian front, he was injured and taken to a hospital in Milan, where he fell in love with a nurse named Agnes von Kurowsky. Although she declined his marriage proposal, these personal experiences seeped into Hemingway's post-war literary career. Published in 1929, *A Farewell to Arms* follows the narrative of the American lieutenant Frederic Henry, who serves in the

Italian ambulance service. Frederic falls in love with an English nurse named Catherine Barkley, who later becomes pregnant. As Hemingway places their romance narrative within a broader wartime context, he therefore gives voice to the individual psychological complexities of people living through the devastating reality of war.

SUMMARY

BOOK ONE: INJURY AND COURTSHIP

Hemingway uses a first-person narrative structure to tell the story of Lieutenant Frederic Henry, an American serving as an ambulance driver in the Italian army. The novel opens with Frederic's description of an Italian village in which he is staying during the summer of 1914. As Frederic describes the physical landscape of the village, Hemingway intersperses this with references to troops and military combat. As such, from the beginning of the novel Frederic's narrative is framed against the backdrop of war. The first chapter skips quickly from "late summer" (p. 3) to "the fall" (*ibid*.) and then into the "start of the winter" (p. 4). Frederic's unit then moves to a town in Gorizia, which has not been badly bombarded. One night, the captain of Frederic's unit mocks the priest about his sexual activity, and two lieutenants then start insulting the priest by attacking religion. As the war is winding down at the onset of winter, Frederic is granted leave and goes on a tour around Italy.

Hemingway does not go into the details of Frederic's leave, but instead jumps forward in time to the following spring, when Frederic "came back to the front" (p. 10). Upon his return, we are introduced to Frederic's friend Lieutenant Rinaldi, who tells Frederic that he is in love with a woman named Miss Barkley. Rinaldi then asks Frederic to lend him some money so he can "make on Miss Barkley the impression of sufficient wealth" (p. 12). Frederic sits next to the priest at dinner, and tells him that his leave consisted of carefree drinking and one night stands. The captain again mocks the priest, but this time he is told to leave him alone by the major. The next morning, Frederic is woken by a battery fire, and goes outside to speak to some of the mechanics working on the ambulance cars. We are told that the division for which Frederic works is planning to attack "at a place up the river" (p. 16), and the ambulances will be stationed as near to the river as possible. Frederic then returns to his room and agrees to meet Miss Barkley with Rinaldi. The pair have a drink and then meet Miss Barkley in the hospital garden, where Frederic speaks with Miss Barkley and Rinaldi with another nurse na-med Helen Ferguson. During their conversation,

Hemingway confirms that Frederic works for the ambulance in the Italian army, and we find out that Miss Barkley works as a nurse. Frederic is struck by her beauty. We also learn that Miss Barkley's fiancé was killed at the Battle of the Somme. Later, Rinaldi remarks that Miss Barkley prefers Frederic to him. The next day, Frederic goes to see Miss Barkley once again, and the reader finds out that her first name is Catherine. Frederic and Catherine kiss. As they continue to meet each other, they become involved in a game of seduction, "like bridge, in which you said things instead of playing cards" (p. 29).

Following an attack by Frederic's division, he is sent up to the river with the ambulances. Before he goes, Catherine gives him her necklace of a metallic Saint Anthony. Once stationed in a dugout near the river, the ambulance drivers discuss the war. As they are eating, their dugout is hit by a shell and Frederic is badly injured. One of his fellow drivers named Passini dies. As Frederic tries to get up, he realises that his kneecap is gone. The surviving drivers then carry Frederic to the medical post, where his wounds are treated. The doctor reports that Frederic has suffered multiple leg and foot wounds, as well as a fracture to the skull. Frederic is then put in an English ambulance and driven to hospital. At the field hospital, Rinaldi visits Frederic and tells him he will receive a silver medal for bravery; the priest then visits Frederic and they discuss the war. It is decided that Frederic will be transferred to a better hospital in Milan the following day. Rinaldi returns with Frederic's major, and they tell him that the Americans are considering declaring war on Germany, and that Catherine is, coincidentally, being transferred to the hospital in Milan. Frederic is then transferred to Milan.

BOOK TWO: USING LOVE AS A DISTRACTION FROM WAR

Frederic arrives at the hospital in Milan and, after some negotiation, gets a room in which he can go to sleep. The reader is introduced to a nurse called Miss Gage, who later informs Frederic that Catherine has arrived in Milan. Frederic and Catherine are reunited, and he then convinces her to have sex with him. Frederic feels that he has fallen in love with her. When Catherine leaves, Miss Gage enters and tells Frederic that

the doctor is on his way to see him. That afternoon, the doctor examines Frederic's leg and
concludes that it will be six months before he
can operate on the knee. Hostile to the idea that
he will have to wait for an operation, Frederic
asks for the opinion of Dr Valentini, who says it
can be operated on tomorrow.

After a successful operation, Catherine and the
other nurses care for Frederic as he recovers.
During the daytime, Catherine and Frederic write
notes to each other, and she works night shifts in
order to spend time with him. Frederic stays at
the hospital all summer, going on carriage rides,
out for dinner and to the races with Catherine.
They relationship becomes very intense and
although they are not legally married, they
consider themselves husband and wife.

As we reach September, the reader learns that
there have been significant losses on both
sides, and especially in the Italian army. Frederic
receives a letter granting him three weeks
convalescent leave, and then he must return to
the front. After he informs Catherine that he is
to return to war, she tells him that she is three
months pregnant. That night, Frederic gets

caught in heavy rain and falls sick with jaundice; however, a nurse named Miss Van Campen finds empty alcohol bottles in his room and accuses him of drinking himself sick. Because of this, Frederic loses his leave. Catherine accompanies Frederic into Turin to board his train back to the front: whilst waiting for the train, they book themselves a hotel room and talk about their baby and how often they will write to each other. They then leave the hotel and Frederic boards a very crowded train.

BOOK THREE: CAPTURE AND ESCAPE

Frederic makes his way back to Gorizia and is told by the major that it has been a bad summer for the war. Back at the front, his first post is to the Bainsizza plateau, located just beyond the place where he was wounded. There is a storm that lasts all afternoon, and at three o'clock in the morning there is a bombardment. After two nights, the German and Austrian troops break the Italian line, and Frederic and with the other drivers begin their retreat to Pordenone. One driver named Bonello picks up two sergeants of engineering en route, whilst Aymo has two girls with him and Piani also accompanies them. Amyo's car later gets stuck in the mud, and when the two sergeants they had been giving a lift refuse to help shift the car, Frederic shoots one of them whilst the other escapes. Unable to get the car moving, they begin to retreat on foot. En route, they come very close to German soldiers, but Frederic is captured and interrogated by the Italian battle police for his 'treachery'. Seeing a possibility to escape, Frederic runs to the river and is carried away from them by the current. Eventually, he climbs onto the bank. He finds a railway line leading from Venice to Trieste, and jumps onto a carriage of a slow-moving train.

BOOKS FOUR AND FIVE: MOMENTARY BLISS FOLLOWED BY TRAGEDY

Frederic gets off the train in Milan, and learns that Catherine left two days ago for Stresa. Having been given some civilian clothes by a man named Simmons, Frederic also leaves for Stresa, where he later finds Catherine. One night, Emilio, who is the bartender at their hotel, tells Frederic that there are people on their way to arrest him for war crimes. Emilio helps Frederic and Catherine escape to Switzerland by boat. They row all night through a storm, but eventually make it across the boarder. They manage to get provisional visas and then go to Montreux. They live privately and happily in each other's company, and learn about the war from the newspapers. Frederic suggests marriage; however, Catherine says that she wants to wait until she has given birth and looks "thin again" (p. 261).

Frederic and Catherine live in the rented chalet throughout January, February and March, but with their baby due within a month they decide to move to the town of Lausanne to be near a hospital. One night, Catherine wakes with contractions and they take a taxi to the hospital. They arrive at the hospital at about three o'clock in the morning, but by two o'clock in the afternoon she still has not given birth. The doctor informs Frederic that the birth has stalled and suggests a C-section. The doctor completes the operation, but their baby was strangled by the umbilical cord and subsequently stillborn. Although Catherine initially survives the opera-

tion, she soon has numerous dangerous haemor-
rhages and passes away. Frederic walks back to
the hotel in the rain.

CHARACTER STUDY

FREDERIC HENRY

Frederic is both the narrator of *A Farewell to Arms* and a character within the narrative. He tells the story in the past tense, privileged with hindsight with regard to how his story progresses and finally concludes; the reader is therefore only allowed knowledge of events that are particularly important to Frederic. As such, we are not told what Frederic looks like or how old he is, and do not actually find out his name until book two. Similarly, we are given few details about his life before the war: we only know that he was based in Rome and was studying to be an architect. Through Hemingway's iceberg style, we can also deduce that he has a strained relationship with his family: in book five, Catherine asks Frederic, "don't you care anything about them?", to which he replies, "I did, but we quarrelled so much it wore itself out." (p. 269).

Given the lack of concrete details about Frederic's life, Hemingway shifts the focus onto his innate psychological complexities. When it comes to his position as an ambulance driver in the war, Frederic the narrator presents himself as someone with a strong sense of moral duty. When Catherine asks him "Why did you join up with the Italians?", Frederic replies, "I was in Italy [...] and I spoke Italian" (p. 21). It therefore seems that for Frederic and his sense of duty, joining the Italian army was the obvious thing to do in a time of conflict. Similarly, Frederic also puts the men in his unit above himself: when stationed at the front in book one, he risks his life by running through a shelling in order to get food to his fellow drivers:

> "'You better wait until the shelling is over'. The major said over his shoulder.
> 'They wish to eat,' I said." (p. 49)

Frederic's response to the major here is expressed in a similar tone to his aforementioned reason for joining the Italian army ("I was in Italy [...] and I spoke Italian"), whereby helping his fellow drivers seems like the only rational thing to do, despite the danger he puts himself in. Moreover, when Frederic is subsequently injured during the shelling, he does not seek praise or martyrdom.

Whilst Rinaldi urges him to seek a silver medal for bravery, Frederic insists that he did not carry out "any heroic act" but was "blown up while we were eating cheese" (p. 59). By distancing himself from romanticised ideas of honour and bravery, Frederic thus presents himself as someone who wants to get the job done out of a sense of duty.

Against this backdrop, Hemingway makes it clear that as the novel progresses, Frederic's clarity of purpose disintegrates. For example, in book three it comes as a shock that Frederic kills one of the engineers when they refuse to help move the car. Given that Frederic's role in the war is to help save people, this episode goes directly against his moral obligations. Furthermore, the section is written in a very matter-of-fact way – "I opened up my holster, took the pistol, aimed at the one who had talked the most, and fired" (p. 182) – and when the men subsequently discuss the murder, they do so with humour. Frederic also takes it as an opportunity to mock religion, claiming "I'll say, 'Bless me, father, I killed a sergeant.'" (p. 186). Furthermore, Frederic goes on to desert the war effort after being interrogated by the Italian police, but rather than thinking about the consequences of this, he is more concerned about the fact that he "would be in a bad position if [he] landed barefoot" (p. 203) on the shore. These episodes highlight Frederic's emotional detachment from the war effort. He seems to feel neither cowardly nor heroic, but just indifferent.

Through Frederic's relationship with Catherine, Hemingway explores Frederic's emotional landscape. Although their relationship starts as a seductive game, they grow to genuinely love one another. Frederic repeatedly displays affection and professes his love for her, and thinks about her constantly when they are apart. However, as Frederic tells his story with hindsight, it becomes clear that he writes with knowledge of the fact that Catherine loses her life in childbirth. He repeatedly refers to the way he treated "seeing Catherine very lightly" (p. 38), reflecting his guilt at not giving her enough attention or spending enough time with her. Similarly, when Catherine dies, Frederic again suffers with guilt at not being able to do anything to help her, as is clear in Hemingway's use of a metaphor about ants:

> "I remember thinking at the time that it was the end of the world and a splendid chance to be a

messiah and lift the log off the fire and throw it out where the ants could get off onto the ground. But I did not do anything but throw a tin cup of water on the log, so that I would have the cup empty to put whiskey in before I added water to it." (p. 290)

His failure to save the ants serves as a metaphor for his inability to help save Catherine's life, although the reader is aware that he could not have done anything anyway. Thus, whilst Frederic seems emotionally numb to the war effort, he invests an abundance of emotion in Catherine, feeling love, loss, guilt and grief.

CATHERINE BARKLEY

Catherine Barkley works as a nurse in the British hospitals, and is introduced to the reader through Frederic's eyes. She is described as "blonde", with "tawny skin and gray eyes", and Frederic thinks she is "very beautiful" (p. 18). Immediately, we find out that she was engaged for eight years to a man she had known all her life, until he was killed when serving at the Somme. As such, when we meet Catherine she is mourning her late fiancé, but also becomes the object of Frederic's affection. There are strong grounds to suggest that Hemingway's portrayal of Catherine is rooted in female stereotypes. When it comes to her relationship with Frederic, she is largely submissive, repeatedly assuring him that she is "good" and will "do anything you want" (p. 96). Furthermore, she regards Frederic as her own personal religion, indicating how she worships him unconditionally. Hemingway continues to draw upon stereotypical representations of women towards the end of the novel when, in pregnancy, she ceases to do anything and becomes a completely passive, metaphorically married housewife. Catherine's willingness to behave passively and her romanticised reverence for Frederic have therefore led many critics to suggest that she is a two-dimensional projection of male fantasy.

However, it is important to be aware of the nuances of her character, which make it more difficult to perceive of Catherine in purely stereotypical terms. Significantly, she works as a nurse, and therefore risks her own life in order to help soldiers as well as the war effort. Furthermore, she is very aware that her relationship with Frederic begins as "a rotten game" (p. 29), and sees through

Frederic when he lies about loving her: "you don't have to pretend you love me" (p. 30). As such, their relationship begins on somewhat equal terms, and Catherine seems far from a fawning stereotype at this stage in the novel. Similarly, she very much holds her own when it comes to marriage. She repeatedly dismisses Frederic's proposals of marriage, asking "what good would it do to marry now [i.e. during the war]?" (p. 103). And whereas Frederic worries about their having a child whilst unmarried, for Catherine this does not seem to be as much of an issue; instead, she is more concerned about marrying when she looks "thin again" (p. 273). Catherine's attitude to marriage therefore goes against social norms, and her metaphorical, rather than legal, marriage to Frederic seems much more important. As such, although Catherine romanticises her relationship with Frederic into a mini-religion, she retains a degree of independence that saves her from becoming a mere two-dimensional stereotype.

RINALDI

Lieutenant Rinaldi is Frederic's closest friend in the novel, and works as a surgeon at the hospital. Through Hemingway's very short description of Rinaldi, we learn that he is "good-looking", about the same age as Frederic and "came from Amalfi" (p. 12). He appears in Frederic's memories of his division, and also visits Frederic whilst he is in hospital recovering from his injuries. Rinaldi is a significant character in the novel due to his ambiguous sexuality. We learn that he regularly sleeps with women in whorehouses, but also frequently kisses Frederic, calls him "baby" (p. 58) and tells him, "I love you too much" (p. 62). Such homoerotic undertones therefore see Hemingway challenge the stereotypical association between masculinity and heterosexuality by celebrating Rinaldi's sexual freedom.

ANALYSIS

NARRATIVE POINT OF VIEW

A Farewell to Arms is written in the past tense, from Frederic's narrative perspective. This means that the reader receives a subjective story that is filtered through Frederic's point of view. As such, the reader only has access to the events that Frederic himself experiences; we therefore do not find out what happens to Rinaldi or the other members of Frederic's division after he deserts to Switzerland. Furthermore, Hemingway encourages the reader to question the reliability of Frederic's narration by having him admit to his lies: for example, in book one Frederic admits that he lies about being in love with Catherine: "'Yes,' I lied. 'I love you.'" (p. 28). Similarly, as Hemingway makes it clear that Frederic is a heavy drinker, we are asked to question the reliability of his memory. Yet despite these factors, *A Farewell to Arms* has a distinctly honest and confessional tone. Frederic does not seek to hide from actions that he may be judged for.

He openly narrates how he committed murder and expresses his guilt for deserting the Italian army; he also confesses that he does not treat Catherine with enough love, and admits that he cannot feel affection towards his new born baby. As such, rather than altering his memories so as to appear in a better light, Frederic seems more concerned with telling the truth of his story, regardless of how it reflects upon his own personal character. Furthermore, given that Frederic tells his story in the past tense, he is aware of the ending whilst narrating the events. As the reader finally learns about the death of Catherine, as well as Frederic's fellow soldiers who were killed whilst serving, the novel can be seen as a memorial for their lives. Consequently, the first person narrative not only communicates Frederic's story; it is also a way of preserving the memory of those he loved and lost.

LOVE VERSUS WAR

The narrative of *A Farewell to Arms* places a romance story in the context of war. As Hemingway stresses the horrific reality of World War I, he portrays love in a highly romanticised, almost illusory way, and therefore contemplates how and whether love can survive in a time of intense conflict. The grotesque nature of fighting is conveyed by Hemingway's shocking description of the bombardment that injures Frederic:

> "I sat up straight and as I did so something inside my head moved like the weights on a doll's eyes and it hit me inside in back of my eyeballs. My legs felt warm and wet and my shoes were wet and warm inside. I knew that I was hit and leaned over and put my hand on my knee. My knee wasn't there. My hand went in and my knee was down on my shin." (p. 51)

The way that Frederic "put [his] hand on [his] knee", only to find that his "knee wasn't there" evokes a deeply grotesque image; meanwhile, the simile "like the weights on a doll's eyes" vividly communicates the severe pain inside his head. Hemingway does not spare the reader from the grim reality of war, but instead uses a blunt style that achieves a matter-of-fact tone. Furthermore, murder is even treated lightly, if not humorously. When Frederic and Bonello murder one of the engineers in book three, they celebrate it with pride. Whilst Bonello boasts "I never killed anybody in this war, and all my life I've wanted to kill a sergeant" (p. 186), Piani also commends the act, saying: "You killed him on the sit all right" (*ibid*.). Furthermore, when Aymo ironically asks "what will you say in confession?" Frederic makes light of the situation by joking, "I'll say, 'Bless me, father, I killed a sergeant'" (*ibid*.). As the sergeant's death is treated humorously, it is clear that the men's capacity for violence is an inevitable consequence of wartime. Hemingway therefore bluntly communicates the spiralling disorder of war to suggest that its horrific reality is unavoidable.

Whilst Hemingway seeks to accurately present the reality of war, Frederic and Catherine's relationship becomes unrealistic and illusory. It begins as a game, which Frederic describes as "like bridge, in which you said things instead of playing cards" (p. 29), thus suggesting that they are playing with the idea of love in order to create their own fictional world. Catherine is outwardly self-conscious of this, pointedly telling Frederic "You don't have to pretend you love me. That's over for the evening" (p. 30). The sentence "that's over for the evening" makes it clear to the reader that their game of love is a way of constructing their own little unreality in order to escape from the grim reality of war. Furthermore, even when their love progresses into something more genuine, they still maintain their fictional reality: for example, they think of themselves as married even though they are not legally married. As such, Hemingway makes it clear that in the reality of war, Frederic and Catherine crave an alternative world of love to which they can escape. However, by the end of the novel Hemingway suggests that unreality cannot be maintained. As Catherine and her child both die during childbirth, the horrors of wartime encroach upon their peaceful, fictional world, and their constructed reality is shattered. As *A Farewell to Arms* concludes rather bleakly, Hemingway therefore suggests that the reality of war is fundamentally inescapable.

CONTRIBUTION TO MODERNISM

Generally speaking, the Modernist period extends from the early 20th century to around 1960, and is regarded as radical, unconventional and experimental in style, form and thinking.

The Modernist movement was born out of the effects of World War I, during a time of global instability, conflict and violence, and the literature of this period consequently reflects the struggle to find meaning in a radically unstable world. Hemingway has come to be classified as part of a group of American writers known as the 'Lost Generation': survivors who were 'lost' in the sense that they were wandering and directionless in the aftermath of WW1. By tuning into the psychological complexities of Frederic Henry, *A Farewell to Arms* encapsulates the deep uncertainty of purpose and meaning in an unstable world that is so common within early Modernist works.

Hemingway's use of the iceberg theory is regarded as a huge contribution to Modernism through its innovation. Hemingway gives the reader a very concise, stripped-back narrative that only scratches the surface of what he is trying to communicate. The rest of Hemingway's meaning, in all its ambiguity, is hidden beneath the words on the page; his style therefore serves as a way of capturing the chaos of the times in which he lived. As an example, Hemingway's theory of omission powerfully communicates the depth of Frederic's anxiety during Catherine's labour:

> "She won't die. She's just having a bad time. The initial labor is usually protracted. She's only having a bad time. Afterwards we'd say what a bad time and Catherine would say it wasn't really so bad. But what if she should die? She can't die. Yes, but what if she should die? She can't, I tell you. Don't be a fool. It's just a bad time." (p. 283)

Without directly telling the reader how Frederic is feeling, Hemingway's use of repetition in this section points towards his inability to move on from the idea that Catherine could die. The repetition of "bad time" is powerful because it suggests that Frederic is in denial of the reality they face, and is instead trying to convince himself that things are not as bad as they seem. Furthermore, Hemingway's subtle movement from "she won't die" to "she can't die" sees Frederic change from an affirmative – "won't" – to more of a desperate plea – "can't". This in turn suggests that there is heavy doubt within Frederic's mind as to whether she will live, although he does not directly make it known. Conjoining this with a staccato rhythm, Hemingway underscores Frederic's narration with a sense of panic, and thus undercuts his affirmation that "she won't die". As such, beneath Hemingway's language lies a wealth of emotion, ambiguities and, in this particular case, an abundance of pain and fear. Radical in its extraordinary style, Hemingway's iceberg theory thus had a huge influence on subsequent Modernist works.

FURTHER REFLECTION

SOME QUESTIONS TO THINK ABOUT...

- How does Hemingway portray the passage of time?
- To what extent is it helpful to consider auto-biographical context in relation to the novel?
- *A Farewell to Arms* was banned from Boston newsstands upon release. Why do you think this is?
- The novel was first adapted for the stage in 1930. How do you think *A Farewell to Arms* might translate to the stage?
- What do you think about Hemingway's presentation of the priest? Explain your answer.
- What is the significance of Catherine's hair?
- Ideas of nationalism and patriotism run through the novel. Comment on this.
- What do you think about the novel's presentation of women?

We want to hear from you!
Leave a comment on your online library
and share your favourite books on social media!

FURTHER READING

REFERENCE EDITION

- Hemingway, E. (1994) *A Farewell to Arms*. Berlin: Arrow Books.

REFERENCE STUDIES

- Parrish, T. (2013) *The Cambridge Companion to American Novelists*. Cambridge: Cambridge University Press.

ADDITIONAL SOURCES

- Dearborn, M.V. (2017) *Ernest Hemingway: A Biography*. London: Penguin Random House.

ADAPTATIONS

- *A Farewell to Arms*. (1957) [Film]. Charles Vidor, John Huston. Dirs. USA: Selznick International Pictures.

- *A Farewell to Arms*. (1932) [Film]. Frank Borzage. Dir. USA: Paramount Pictures.

MORE FROM BRIGHTSUMMARIES.COM

- Reading guide – *A Moveable Feast* by Ernest Hemingway.

- Reading guide – *For Whom the Bell Tolls* by Ernest Hemingway.

- Reading guide – *The Old Man and the Sea* by Ernest Hemingway.

Although the editor makes every effort to
verify the accuracy of the information published,
BrightSummaries.com accepts no responsibility for
the content of this book.

www.brightsummaries.com

Ebook EAN: 9782808012867

Paperback EAN: 9782808012874

Legal Deposit: D/2018/12603/399

Cover: © Primento

Digital conception by Primento, the digital partner of
publishers.

Made in the USA
Columbia, SC
12 June 2022

61648036R00033